M1
North
BRENT X
LONDON
hampstead heath
Archway Rd.
park
REGENT'S
CANAL
Camden Road
SIMON COMMUNITY
CAMDEN TOWN
High St.
SQUAT
SUNSET STRIP
ST. PANCRAS
KING'S CROSS
Regent's park
Euston Road

DEER ISLAND

DEER ISLAND

Neil Ansell

Illustrated by
Jonny Hannah

Little Toller Books
DORSET

The Drift

2013

IT IS SPRING and the herring gulls have staked their claim on the roof opposite. There are six pairs evenly spaced along the length of the block, and I know there are more pairs that I can't see on my own roof. They start calling at first light, from a conversational quickfire cackling to a full-on heads-back beaks-wide yodelling that used to wake me every morning when I first moved here. Now I hardly notice it.

From my window I can just make out a little sliver of grey ocean between the buildings. You could hardly warrant calling it a sea view, though an estate agent probably would. I did much of my growing up in sight of the sea so it is nice to know it is there. Walking to the beach takes about five minutes. At first I walked down to the sea almost every day, and imagined that I always would, but of course in time I began to take it more and more for granted, until I had almost forgotten it was there, at least when it was not obvious beach weather. It's not going anywhere, after all. Sometimes though I still surprise myself and take a solitary walk along the tideline. I walk away from the tinkling and chuntering of the fairground rides and arcades, away from the perfume of vinegar and candyfloss. Perhaps I will see something unexpected, a storm-blown gannet or a phalarope bobbing in the waves. I comb the flotsam of the latest storm, and the shingle makes a satisfying crunch beneath my feet, and the surf smells clean and bright, and I think to myself: Why don't I do this more often? If I rise early I may even have the beach to myself, and stroll absentmindedly along picking up things that catch my eye – fairy stones and mermaids' purses, shards of driftwood smoothed by waves and garish tangles of fishing twine or shreds of lost nets. And when I get home I unload my pockets, wondering why I have all these things, and add them to the drift that has accumulated on my kitchen windowsill, alongside the fragments of coral and exotic seashells that I have brought back from tropical shores.

Now that the herring gulls have paired up they don't wander far. A lot of the time they seem to spend on the grassy bank at the edge of the estate, doing their gull dance. With a look of apparent concentration, they drum their big flappy webbed feet on the ground as rapidly as they can, and this seems to be remarkably effective at bringing up worms and bugs that they can gobble down. They also have a habit of ripping open any bin bags left out overnight and picking through the contents. A lot of people complain about them, but not everyone dislikes them; some people persist in putting out food for them in spite of, or perhaps because of, the letters from the council asking them to desist. Personally I don't mind the gulls. This is the seaside, and our rooftops are just cliffs to them. They probably belong here more than I do.

I find it hard to believe that I have been in Brighton for so long. It was not really my intention; I never thought I would stay anywhere for long. It feels as though I just washed up here by accident, stranded, like driftwood. When I tell people that I have travelled in the best part of a hundred countries they sometimes ask me to name a favourite place. It is an impossible choice – how do you compare beach with mountaintop, rainforest with desert? But if pushed I will often surprise people by saying somewhere closer to home: the Isle of Jura.

It is a place that I cannot forget, because I have left a little piece of myself there, a fragment of who I am. In particular I think of a little storm-lashed promontory on the uninhabited west coast of the island. I always thought that I would go back there again, and perhaps I still will. Yet somehow over twenty years have passed since the last time I was there.

It was morning as I walked along the rocks. I had been walking this coast alone for days, sleeping under the stars or in empty bothies, building driftwood fires each night. It was spotting with rain; I could see the rain clouds moving in from the western horizon. As I looked out beyond the small islands of Colonsay and Oronsay I could see just open ocean; there was nothing else between here and Canada. I sat down behind a pile of rocks, the only shelter from the gusting wind. I began to wonder whether this was an ancient cairn built in memory of the long-ago dead, or if it had simply been accumulated here by passing walkers, rock by rock.

I decided that this would be the place. Remote,

isolated. I can still picture the spot perfectly, a place where the otters play. I began to dismantle the little cairn; to find its heart, and then to rebuild it with my talisman at its core. I could not have explained quite why I was doing what I was doing, not to myself let alone to others. But sometimes a symbolic gesture is all that we have to give.

Sunset Strip

1980

I HAD BEEN in London for less than a week when I was taken on a visit to Sunset Strip. I was the guest of two homeless people called Peggy and Woodsy. Peggy was a lively and friendly young woman from Belfast. Though she was only in her early twenties she already had the flushed face of a hardened drinker. Woodsy was a tall, craggy Scotsman in his fifties. He walked with a cane and was wrapped in an old donkey jacket against the autumn wind.

We arrived at dusk, as people were coming in off the street, starting to think about where they might spend the night. Sunset Strip was the name everyone gave to a long-standing row of derries on a back street in Camden Town – derries being derelict buildings rather than squats; no water, no electricity, no locks. Just a roof, really. A place of last resort.

We walked to the last house on the terrace. There was

no door, but a sheet of corrugated iron that we had to bend back to get inside. In the hallway the floorboards were all gone, with only the joists remaining, and I took Woodsy's arm to help support him. I supposed that the floorboards had all been ripped up to go on the fire. Scraps of torn wallpaper hung from the walls, damp and mould-stained. We turned into the front room and it took me a moment to become accustomed to the dark. There was no window; like the doorway the space had been filled with corrugated iron. A couple of candles were burning on the mantelpiece, and there was a small fire in the grate.

Casey was slumped in front of the fire in an old armchair with its stuffing spilling out in all directions. He turned to greet us without rising but with a friendly smile, and shook my hand gravely when we were introduced. He was a big man, wearing an open-necked shirt and with a chunky crucifix around his neck. He looked pale and wan, and like he was overcome by tiredness. Casey was a Belfast Catholic, Peggy a Protestant; the Troubles were raging on in Northern Ireland, but here on the streets what people had in common seemed more important than their differences.

It was as if they had thrown any sectarianism overboard on the ferry from Larne. People never talked about their past. It was best that way.

I volunteered to go out and raid a nearby skip for extra firewood, and when I got back other people had started to gather, about a dozen of them. They all sat on the floor around the walls, with their bottles by their side. Apart from Casey's armchair, there was no other furniture in the room save for a single mattress in the corner, and no one sat on that. I was told that Casey's partner had died on that mattress two weeks earlier, so it would have been disrespectful. I recognised one of the new arrivals: John was a tall Irishman with jet black hair and a black suit that had long since seen better days. He was a quiet man, but on the infrequent occasion when he did speak, he spoke with charm. There were two more people expected, and they arrived soon after. Gypsy Davy gave me a wink of acknowledgement, and Scots Mary was loud and feisty after a day spent drinking on the street. And then our party was complete.

Everybody had brought bottles of VP wine or cooking sherry. These people were winos, by their own description. I was starting to find my way around the different tribes on the street. The beer drinkers looked down on the cider drinkers, and the cider drinkers scorned the winos. The winos had no time for the jakies, and the jakies. . . well, most of the time the jakies lived in a place beyond speech, but even they, in their most lucid moments, would say: At least I'm not a junkie. And the junkies would look at the drinkers and consider them somewhat déclassé, for needing to pour pints of liquid down their throats in order to seek their oblivion, when all you needed was a millilitre of liquid gold, and a vein.

There were rules. Though everyone had brought a bottle, they were not all opened at once. Rather, there would only be one in circulation at any one time and it would be shared, passed around the entire company. Casey was the host so it was up to him to kick things off. He unscrewed the first bottle and took a deep gulp, then paused for a moment as if considering, before passing it deliberately to me. I think it was his way of saying that although I was a stranger to most, I was his guest and should be made to feel welcome. This was my induction into the world of the homeless.

It had not been a plan so much as a whim. I had met someone who had worked with street homeless people in London, for a small charity called The Simon Community. I had listened to her stories, and had been drawn to what sounded like the sheer bloody-minded extremity of the place. The Community had been founded in the 1960s with the avowed intention of working with people for whom there was no other provision; the hardcore long-term rough sleepers, the jakies or crude spirit drinkers. It was not overtly aiming for rehabilitation; rather it tried to provide a safe space where people, any people, whatever their problems, could be accepted on their own terms. It stubbornly refused to take any government funding; instead it chose to operate on a shoestring, begging and borrowing and muddling along as best it could. There were no paid staff, just untrained volunteers who mucked in with the Community's homeless residents and did their best.

I first went for a weekend visit; to see how I liked the place, and how the place liked me. It was chaos, but it seemed to thrive on that chaos. The Community had three houses; a short-stay place in Camden Town, a headquarters in Kentish Town, where some residents had been living for years, and a farmhouse high on the north downs of Kent, which had some residents who'd stayed for over a decade. But much of the work was geared towards those still on the outside. I stayed up the whole of my first night making hundreds of jam sandwiches and filling urns with gallons of sugary tea, and before dawn a group of us set off in a battered Transit van and headed down to the West End. I found myself face to face with a world that would not have looked unfamiliar to George Orwell, whose *Down and Out in Paris and London* had depicted life on the streets fifty years earlier.

Cardboard City. Under the shadow of the Hungerford bridge, by Embankment tube station, around a hundred and fifty people, nearly all men, were lined up along the wall in cardboard boxes. Trains rumbled and roared repeatedly overhead, sending flurries of pigeons into the air that would settle again a few moments later. In the middle of the long row of cardboard, a man was sleeping in a wheelchair. He had lost both legs to frostbite, but was still here. Although it was not yet light, there was already a long queue of people who were up and waiting for us. As our van pulled up they clustered around us, reaching out for plastic cups of tea. I was given the job of dispensing tobacco. I would hand them a single cigarette paper, then fill it with a pinch of Old Holborn. Some men's hands were shaking too badly to roll their own, and I had to make their cigarettes for them. People grumbled about the 'dossers' who had not slept here but had spent the night in a hostel or shelter, and had risen early to get a place in the queue.

We walked the line of cardboard where people still slept and began to wake them with offers of tea. The police would be along shortly anyway, with the bin men close behind gathering up the cardboard to be taken to the tip, and then the water wagon would come and hose down the pavements. This was a city of the night. It would all be swept away, obliterated, before the first commuters started arriving at the station for their day's work.

We visited other places that morning. At the back of the Strand Palace Hotel, vents from the basement boiler rooms sent out gusts of warm air at pavement level, and people jostled for the best positions. At the casual labour exchange at Mortimer Street, homeless people who could still muster up a thin veneer of respectability and a clean white shirt would camp out all night in the hope of being offered a shift as a KP – a kitchen porter – washing dishes or peeling potatoes in a hotel kitchen. As the sun rose we made our way to our last port of call: Lincoln's Inn Fields was a small oasis of green surrounded by law firms. A local bye-law decreed that it had to remain open twenty-four hours a day, and many people slept there in the bandstand or under the bushes. At dawn every morning they would build a bonfire of the night's cardboard, and we joined them around the fire, drinking tea and chatting.

The Community was a place of ingrained traditions; for twenty years it had tried to stay close to its founding principles, the house meetings after breakfast each day, the soup every lunchtime as a daily reminder of those who were still out there and living on soup alone, the open-door hospitality that could result in queues of people stretching down the road. The charity's founder had died not long before, suddenly and unexpectedly, and had left the place somewhat rudderless, but his absence was not regarded as an opportunity to make changes; quite the reverse. He still cast a long, long shadow over the place, and his name was constantly invoked, almost reverentially. The Community's default position was: If it was good enough for Anton, then it's good enough for us.

No one was paid, and everyone was expected to contribute to the best of their ability. The volunteers were a mix of mostly young idealists – like me, I suppose – plus a handful of foreign students who had come with the intention of improving their English and often had little idea of what they were letting themselves in for, and a rather larger number of formerly homeless residents who had stayed on as volunteers. With such a porous boundary between resident and volunteer, there was a risk of traffic the other way too, and there were cautionary tales of people who had come as volunteers, and ended up on the streets themselves. The beds were generally all full, so the volunteers camped on the floor space between beds or in the offices. You were never alone, not for a minute of the day. It was a curious life, but one that immersed you totally. Though in some ways we were politically and socially engaged, in other respects it was a bubble, a world all of its own. In the time I spent there I don't suppose I ever read a newspaper, or watched a television programme, or listened to a new song on the radio. I never had the time.

The Community's precept of voluntary poverty appealed to me. I soon found that it was not only possible but actually liberating to live with no possessions whatsoever. I had food and shelter, and if I needed clothes there was a donated pile to choose from; enough that often we would have to have a clear-out, and take the surplus to the East End rag-traders to sell by the van-load. At the end of each day we would visit the couple of supermarkets that donated their sell-by dated food to us. What we got would depend on the vagaries of their stock-ordering system. We might get a van full of tomatoes, and nothing else. On one occasion, in the run-up to Christmas, I remember us coming away with several van-loads of ready salted crisps.

I started off in the Community's 'first-tier' house in Camden, in the hinterland of gasometers and railway sidings at the back of King's Cross station. Here, people came and went, often just staying for a night or two. We tried not to turn people away; if the beds were full, which they generally were, we gave them blankets and invited them to sleep on sofas or on the living room floor. There were only two rules: no violence and no bottles. Intoxication was not a problem in itself; people could just hand their bottles to us at the door, along with any semi-legal drugs like barbiturates or tranquillisers, and we would hand them back when they went out. We would try to find alternative accommodation for people if they wanted, and by default would end up with a group of longer-term residents who were hard to place. It was not hard to find yourself ineligible for almost any hostel in London; by not being ready and willing to go dry; by being one half of a couple that didn't want to be split up; by having a dog. There were hostels in London that conducted a sniff-test at the door, and if you smelt of alcohol you would be summarily excluded. When beds became available in the other houses we would move people up through the system if they were deemed suitable. By suitable I mean completely unsuitable to go anywhere else.

The house was in a little isolated terrace that was

scheduled for demolition, wedged between a railway bridge and a road bridge over the Regent's Canal. It was perfectly situated between predominantly Irish Camden Town and the Scottish heartland that was King's Cross. It was here that I met Peggy and Woodsy who would take me for my visit to Sunset Strip. Peggy had come back with us on the tea-run on my very first day; Woodsy was an old regular.

A few days after my visit to Sunset Strip I walked that road again; I was accompanying Peggy down to the social and it was on our way. Casey was sat alone on the steps outside his derry, bathing in the weak rays of the winter sun, his bottle by his side, and he invited us to sit with him for a while. As we sat on the steps with him and chatted, a young man approached us and asked if he could take our photo. We agreed, for the price of a bottle. I wonder now what he wanted our photograph for, and what became of it. I would never see Casey again, he died soon after. He passed away less than a month after the death of his partner, as if he could not bear to go on without her. And when I thought back to the little time I had spent with him, I imagined that I could see that resignation in his eyes, and wondered if it would have been preserved, there, in that photograph.

Not long after that Sunset Strip burned to the ground. The whole terrace was gone. And when Peggy moved on, we lost touch. People came and went all the time; it was a nebulous, drifting world. You would find someone crossing your mind, and realise you hadn't seen them for a while, and wonder what had become of them. As often as not you would never find out. I don't know what became of Peggy, but she was still young, and I like to think she might have made it. John didn't make it; charming Irish John who was still in his early thirties. He was part of a school that spent their drinking days on the benches along the towpath, beside the turbid waters of the Regent's Canal. One night he didn't show up back at the house, but that was not unusual. In their cups, people would often just end up sleeping wherever the night found them. Or perhaps he was having a night in the drunk tank; that would not be unusual either. But the next morning he was found floating face-down in the canal. There was never any explanation.

I was outside the house one morning when I saw

Woodsy walking slowly up the road towards me. He was struggling, he looked defeated. As he drew closer I could see the blood on his neck, like he had been bitten by a vampire. Woodsy was a hard man, but there was horror in his eyes, a thousand-yard stare. I asked him what had happened, and he showed me the blood that dripped from his sleeve, the bloodstains that bloomed like roses on his shirt and his trouser leg. He had spent the night alone in the underground car park, sleeping the dreamless sleep of the deeply inebriated. When he had finally woken, he had found himself covered in rats. Rats the size of cats, he told me. He thanked god that he had his stick with him.

I took him straight to the hospital to get his wounds treated. He was discharged the same day, but it was the beginning of the end for Woodsy. His TB escalated and he had to be admitted. TB was virtually extinct in the wider population, but on the streets it was still rife. It should be relatively easy to treat with courses of antibiotics, but I suppose that the lifestyle of a street drinker is not conducive to remembering to take your medication consistently. There was a whole segregation ward at the nearby Hospital for Tropical

Diseases dedicated to those suffering from TB, and there would always be people there that I knew.

When I went to visit Woodsy, Gypsy Davy and Mary were there. They had smuggled in a bottle and were sharing it with him. Many of Woodsy's drinking companions would spend the day there keeping him company, at least until they were thrown out. So at least he didn't die alone. Woodsy was over six feet tall, but by the end there was not much left of him, and he weighed only a few stone.

Of those who I knew from my visit to Sunset Strip, only Davy and Mary were left now. They were both Scottish Gypsy-Travellers who had arrived in Camden Town some thirty years earlier. They had met there, and had been together ever since. They were a proper old couple, treating one another with that perfect balance of tenderness and scorn. They were notorious beggars in Camden, and I would often go and visit them at their pitch by the tube station. Mary was the main breadwinner, working the street while Davy sat in a doorway. I would join him and sit and chat while we watched Mary doing what she did best. She was hard to resist, with her straggly hair that had long since passed grey and was now a perfect white, her gap-toothed smile and her wheedling voice. But woe betide anyone who gave her any grief; she could give far better than she got, and could turn the air blue with her cusses. Gypsy Davy was a small wiry man, wrinkled and almost completely bald, and with skin tanned to leather. He was a charmer, one of those drinkers given to ruefully summing up the world in thoughtful epigrams; a street philosopher.

Mary would often stay with us when she felt the need for a break from the street, with hot meals, hot water, a change of clothes, but Gypsy Davy almost never would. The only time he would come back was when he was too ill to do otherwise. I would sit with him and try to persuade him to go to hospital. No, son, he would say, shaking his head sadly. Hospitals are for dying in. And perhaps Davy knew what he was talking about; when he was finally too ill to say no to an ambulance, he was dead of pneumonia within days.

For some reason, all the times I met up with Gypsy Davy and Scots Mary in the street, Davy would not try to beg off me, and nor would he allow Mary to. Mary had a catholic approach to begging otherwise; no man, woman or child was safe from her attentions. I didn't know what I had done to earn such an exemption. It couldn't have been self-interest on Gypsy Davy's part; I had nothing that he wanted.

The average stay for volunteers at the Community was just three months, but in the end I would spend three years there. I left, finally, because I was worn out; worn out from years of sleeping on floors and never having a moment to myself, but most of all worn out from making friends with people and then having to watch them die.

Deer Island

1984

I HAD EVERYTHING I needed in life: a companion, a tent and a motorbike. Liz had been working as a volunteer with me, and together we were planning a trip to her home in Sweden. But first we wanted to spend six months of the summer touring Britain, as she had hardly been out of London. The tent, just a little two-man thing, was our leaving present. They got us out of the house on some pretext and when we returned there it was, fully erected, with nails in lieu of tent pegs hammered into the floorboards. The Simon Community may not have paid its workers, but for long-stayers it did give you a token payment when you departed, a leaving allowance, on the very reasonable assumption that you would probably be totally unfit for work for quite some time.

We hitchhiked up to Newcastle to visit friends, and there I spent virtually all my leaving money on a beast of a bike, an all-black Triumph Bonneville that was very nearly as old as me. Then we were set. We didn't want to stay long in the city, but a couple of old friends of mine were renting a cottage in Northumberland, by the edge of the moors, right by Hadrian's Wall, and we made that our home base, between their vegetable patch and their flower bed. From there we made forays out into the countryside, camping wild wherever we found ourselves. A week or so exploring the coast of Northumberland, to Lindisfarne and up to the Scottish border, camping on empty beaches, and then across to the Lake District, following the high road over the Pennines through Alston, a road full of switchbacks, and full of bikers riding just for the joy of it. After all the time we had spent surrounded by others, sleeping in rooms full of people, we revelled in the freedom of it, and the privacy.

An old British bike like that was probably more suited to someone with a better grasp of roadside repairs than me. At speed it would start to judder and shake, nuts and bolts would work loose and fly past my ear, and I would have to pull over and try to find them on the verge, then work out where they belonged. Not everything was found though. It was a pretty basic bike as it was, without even any indicators, but as time passed it became gradually more and more basic. First I lost my side-stand, and then I lost my centre-stand; to park it I would need to find a wall to lean it against. A group of bikers had squatted a house and garage in a nearby village and set up a workshop, so we spent quite a bit of our time hanging with them and tinkering. While my bike was off the road they would lend me whatever they had lying around; a little trail bike for a while, a BSA, and finally a Cossack. This bike, dubbed the urinal, was ridiculously heavy and slow even by comparison with my Triumph. I would amuse myself with the fact that it had a reverse gear, and the sidecar had been removed.

Our trips up the coast and across to the Lakes had just been dummy runs, really, for the main event; we were heading for Scotland. I had hitched around Scotland before with a former girlfriend, sleeping rough as we went, and made it to Mull and Skye and a couple of the small islands. I had no particular destination in mind until one of the friends whose garden we were staying in recommended the Isle of

Jura; wild, with very few people, and not too far north. He had been to most of the islands and said that was his favourite.

We drove west, following the wall, crossing the country to Carlisle before turning north and entering Scotland at Gretna Green. Somewhere in the Borders south of Glasgow the clutch went. I powered on regardless, just stamping it through the gears; not too bad if you get the timing right, but of course if I stopped I stalled, and the kick start had gone with the clutch and hung slack and useless. A push start, running alongside the bike and then jumping on, was never going to happen with a pillion-passenger plus a tent and pack strapped on the back. The only way was to freewheel downhill, then send the bike juddering back to life, which was all very well if we stopped on a downhill slope; if we had to stop on a rise I would have to turn the bike round, paddle it downhill and then do a U-turn.

It was the Great Western Road out of Glasgow that finally defeated me. For mile after mile it rose, and along it were twenty-seven sets of traffic lights – I know because I counted them. Finally, we stopped and leaned the bike against a roadside wall, sat on the pavement and waited. The advantage of having a classic bike is that it draws people's attention; they come and look and talk to you all the time. First up were a couple of grizzled bikers, who pulled over and jotted down an address for a British bike workshop a couple of miles out of town. Then a couple of teenage lads stopped in a car. They said we could stay with them that night and they would take us round the breakers' yards in the morning. We shrugged and said sure, why not?

That night they took us round the bars and clubs. They warned me to stay close and keep my voice down; this was a hard town, they told me. It seemed that I had been told this wherever I went, that the place I was in was too dangerous for me, and I would be a provocation. This is what they had said in Belfast; this is what they had said in Harlem; this is what they had said in Bogotá. Yet it seemed to me that if you treated people with respect and didn't go asking for trouble, then you didn't get it. Perhaps I had just been lucky. But I didn't say anything; they were our hosts and they meant well. Years of working with street drinkers and junkies had not dented my conviction that people were essentially good, and that, given the chance to do the right thing, they would always take it.

We spent the morning touring the breakers' yards of Glasgow, but to no avail. In the end I asked the boys to drop us back at the bike, and then I pushed it miles further out of town to the address I had been given, jumping on and freewheeling on a rare downhill stretch. The guy at the workshop could not have been more helpful; he dropped what he was doing, and said he would sort it while we waited, to get us back on the road before nightfall. It would have taken days to order the parts we needed, so he stripped what he could from an old Triumph Tiger he was in the middle of renovating, and did the job at cost. He had been in the same situation many times himself, he told us, far from home and reliant on the kindness of strangers.

And then we were away, making up for lost time, unwinding the miles, heading for the Highlands, on a road that wrapped itself around the shores of Loch Lomond. Geography meant we had to travel well to the north of our destination, and then turn south onto the peninsula of Kintyre to head for the ferry port at

Kennacraig. It was good to be moving again, and the sun kept shining into the evening. There would be no more ferries that day; we camped out there for the night to await the first ferry of the day.

The morning ferry took us to Port Ellen on the south coast of Islay. It was a two hour crossing, and we whiled away the time leaning on the rail and watching the storm petrels that pattered in our wake. They looked too frail, too dainty, to be seabirds, dwarfed by the swell of the waves. They dabbled their feet in the water without ever quite settling, dancing across the face of the waters. Perhaps it was this restlessness, this weightlessness, that led to the old seafarers' belief that they were the souls of the drowned, Mother Carey's chickens; Mother Carey being the female version of Davy Jones.

The Islay ferry alternated between the south and north of the island, so we had to cross the island for the final leg of our journey. There was a long road, straight and narrow, across the heart of the island. It was like a racetrack, and I could see there was no traffic at all, so I couldn't resist. I picked up speed, faster and faster, as fast as my old bike would go. We hit a little humpback bridge over a stream, and we were flying.

It is only a narrow stretch of water, the Sound of Islay that divides the two islands, just a five minute crossing, but it is like a gateway to another world. Jura looked bleak, remote and wild; it made Islay look fertile and populous in comparison. It was an appealing prospect; there is nothing better than looking into the wilderness and knowing you are going there. Jura is not a small island; it is thirty miles from north to south and ten miles across, yet it has a population of less than two hundred, most of whom live in the island's one small village. The name Jura comes from the Old Norse and means deer island. There are five thousand red deer on its hills – twenty-five deer for every person – that keep the moors grazed and the island virtually treeless. There is just one solitary road, single-tracked, with a strip of grass growing down the middle that starts from the ferry landing on the south of the island and clings to the relatively sheltered east coast, finally giving up about ten miles short of the island's northern tip. The west of the island is completely trackless and uninhabited.

I rode onto the little ferry with a couple of cars, and the ferryman came over to admire my bike. They don't make them like that any more, he said. True, I thought, for good and for bad. I let the cars disembark first and then we slowly made our way along the coast road, savouring the scenery and the unexpected afternoon sunshine.

The village of Craighouse has one hotel, one post office-cum-store-cum-tearoom, and one distillery. We stopped off there for supplies, campfire food, and then headed on to look for a suitable spot to overnight. There was not much shelter, just heather on the high hills and bracken on the lower slopes. In the south of the island there had been a few small plantations of conifers, but here was almost bare.

After five or ten miles we spotted a little copse of birches down towards the shore. There were no houses at all in view, and it was far enough off the road to be perfectly secluded. I propped the bike against a wooden waymarker. We unloaded and waded through the chest-high bracken to our chosen place.

It was a perfect spot, sheltered and with sufficient dead wood to get a fire going. After all the travelling we decided to spend two nights here, and have a day on foot. It was a lazy day, strolling along the shoreline around a rocky headland. There was a herd of wild goats on the crags that seemed impossible to reach. They were small and shaggy, and all different colours. These are not native animals but might as well be: they have been here, running wild, for so long. They are not much like our domesticated goats; these are an ancient breed, a breed that would have come with the earliest arrivals on our shores.

A circling golden eagle, slab-like in the sky, came in lower, and lower, sending the goats skittish. It was probably looking for an unaccompanied kid, but the young wisely stayed close. Later in the day the red deer began to come down off the hill. They would spend the day on the high moors but would descend to lower ground towards evening, to drink from the streams or to forage on the tideline. It seems odd to see deer on a beach, but they are actually surprisingly good swimmers; a trip to the mainland would not be beyond them.

Finally we rounded the headland and found ourselves in a little bay with a single house on the shore. We followed the shoreline back to the road that would lead us back to our campsite, and got the fire going for dinner. After we had eaten I left Liz by the fireside and headed back down to the rocky shore alone. The sun had already fallen behind the hills and left me in shadow, but across the waters the west coast of Kintyre was still lit up by the last dying rays of sunset, and I sat and looked out, tired from the day's walking but at peace. I saw a movement in the mat of bladderwrack and kelp washed up at the water's edge. It was an otter, my first. It seemed to materialise out of nowhere; one moment the beach had been deserted and then suddenly it was there, not ten feet away from where I sat on my rock. I supposed it had risen stealthily from the water. It seemed oblivious to my presence so close by; though perhaps more likely it knew perfectly well that I was there, and didn't mind. Its fur was all spiky and tufted from the wet, and it scoured the waterline restlessly, scrabbling away at the seaweed in search of morsels to eat. Its whiskers twitched constantly, and it never paused, never stopped moving for a second. It seemed more vital, more fully alive than almost any creature I had seen before; a charge of electricity ran through it. I stayed as motionless as I could, tried to slow my breathing, to step out of time. I watched it through sunset and into the gloaming; I watched it until it was too dark to see. And then I slipped away, waded back through the bracken to the clump of birches that was now just a shadow against the sky.

In the morning we packed up our tent. The plan was to head to the far north of the island and cross to the wild west coast. But the bike wouldn't start; I spent an hour trying to get it going but it remained completely lifeless. Eventually a car came by, heading south, and we hitched a ride to the village. In the shop I asked if there was a workshop on the island, or at least anyone who knew something about bikes. There was one man on the island, the woman told me, but he was away.

In the teashop attached to the store there was a single customer, a young woman who called us over. Is that your bike parked up the road there? she asked. I'm your nearest neighbour. It turned out she lived in the little house on the bay we had passed on our walk the previous afternoon. She told us her story; she had moved here from London to start a new life with her husband and their four children. Her husband was a roofer, and was sure there would be enough work on the island to keep them. But there wasn't, and he'd had to move back to the mainland to make a living, leaving her and the kids stranded here. She invited us to stay with her; I could work on the bike in her barn, take as long as I needed.

So that's what we did. We jumped in her car and she dropped me off so I could push the bike the last mile or two up to hers. Liz stayed in chatting to the woman, who talked and talked; I suppose she was bored and lonely and desperate for adult conversation. Meanwhile I spent my day in the barn, staring accusingly at the bike, as if I could browbeat it into submitting to my will. I had only the most basic of tool kits, an even more basic knowledge of the workings of an internal combustion engine, and of course no realistic access to any parts without having to wait for days or even weeks. All I knew was that abandoning the bike here and returning for it later would make life too complicated.

I took out the plugs and cleaned them and tested

them. They were both sparking. This was a relief; if it had been an electrical problem it would have taken me into a whole new world of ignorance. I supposed that if it wasn't the electrics then it was most likely the fuel supply. I took off the carburettor and dismantled it, spreading out all its tiny component parts on a rag like an exploded diagram from a motor manual. Then I carefully washed them all out with petrol, reassembled them and put the bike back together. To my astonishment it worked, and the bike burst back into life.

Liz and I sat on the strand and considered our options. We could stay on and hope that the bike held out until we were ready to leave, or we could take advantage of this window of opportunity and go before the bike had a chance to break down again. Reluctantly, we accepted that we should get going while we knew that we could, and packed up and headed for the ferry. I knew that one day I would return. This was a new experience for me; I had never previously considered the possibility of going back to a place I had already been, when the world was so vast and so full of places I had yet to see.

I have two photographs of myself with the bike on Jura, in which I can hardly recognise myself. I certainly look the part; long hair, beard, black leather jacket, original jeans and steel-capped work boots. The bike looks imposing too, big and black and shiny, though it would have looked even more impressive without the gaffer tape holding it together. These are the oldest photos I have in my possession; in fact they are the only photos I have from the first half of my life. I guess that Liz must have posted them on to me, years later, after we had split up.

Empty Rooms

1988

IF I TELL PEOPLE of my love of mountains, they understand me immediately; they may not share my feelings, but they at least understand their origin. Yet when I try to explain to people the allure of deserts, I am as often as not met by a look of total incomprehension. In my travels I have hitchhiked across the deserts of the American southwest and the north of Mexico, and across the Nullarbor plain in Australia. I have likewise travelled through the Sahara and the Atacama. When you travel you are in search of otherness, and what could be more other than a desert? It is landscape stripped bare, free of the markers of familiarity, inimical of life. I prided myself on being a good traveller; I would always say that I felt at home wherever I was, because I carried my home with me, my home was in my head. I would never feel that the place I had come to was remote;

instead it had become the centre of my own personal world. Sometimes everywhere else was remote. And so I would seek out the wildest of wild places, always pushing myself to go a little further, as if to test my feelings of self-sufficiency to their utmost.

But I think I lost my way a little in the Kalahari, and misplaced a part of myself. I was hitchhiking alone across the desert on a rutted dirt track that led across the Makgadikgadi salt pans, and it was the most extreme landscape I had ever seen. The silence was total and there was no sign of any living thing. The land was stretched perfectly flat and unmarked to every horizon. Except there was no horizon, because the heat haze melded the earth to the sky in an unbroken wash of light. The pans were the bed of a shallow lake long since dried up, leaving just salt. The earth was a crystal plain, entirely featureless. It was a pristine place, a primal place, a place that seemed to have no beginning and no end, no past and no future.

In the late afternoon a vehicle arrived at last, a flatbed truck. There were already about a dozen people on top with their sacks and boxes and livestock. I gave the driver a few pula, as was the custom here, and climbed up with the others. It pleased me that here in Botswana, a country blessed with such a wealth of mineral resources, the local currency was named after the Setswana word for rain. It made me feel that the people here knew the true value of things.

We set off painfully slowly to the west, lurching into hundreds of miles of desert, the truck pitching and yawing on the terrible road. We were driving into a desert storm, a huge black tower of cloud that seemed to touch the ground and stretched all the way into the heavens. Pinpricks of forked lightning were touching down all around us; you could feel the electricity in the air. As the first drops of rain fell, there were gasps from the truck; the raindrops were huge and icy cold. And then a moment later we were in the thick of it. The young man facing me pointlessly pulled up his T-shirt to cover his head; he glanced up at me and we caught each other's eye, and we began to laugh. The freezing rain was torrential, there was no possible way of keeping any part of yourself dry; all you could do was surrender yourself to it in its entirety.

I think a part of me was washed away by that rainstorm in the desert. I felt that I no longer had any will, any power of self-determination, that I no longer had any control over my future, that any choices I could make were an irrelevance, that I was in the hands of the universe and I could only follow wherever it might lead me. After an hour or two we passed through the storm, with just a little horizontal light remaining before nightfall. Everyone was shivering, and looked a little shocked and in awe, like the survivors of a tragedy. We were rewarded by an extraordinary purple sunset, a sunset such as I had never seen in my life before. At the roadside was the first living creature I had seen in hours. A gemsbok with scimitar horns several feet long stood facing across the road, perfectly erect and immobile, like a sentry on duty. Its pelt was steaming and in the evening light its shadow stretched out far across the plain. The sight of life, and the sight of a shadow, was almost shocking.

I returned from Africa a few months later with no money, no job prospects and nowhere to live. Most of the past five years I had spent away, working when I could or just keeping moving when I couldn't. On the few occasions I had returned briefly to England, my goal had been to work as hard as I could and spend as little as I could, to save some seed money to get going again. But for now at least I felt travelled out and was without ambition; I had no idea what I would do with myself. To save enough money for the deposit on a room would take time and a job, so to start with I just travelled around visiting friends, sofa-surfing. But I knew I could not do this for long, for I had learned that the first rule of accepting hospitality is always to move on before you have outstayed your welcome. I knew that I would have to squat.

The first place I took was an empty council flat in London. It was on the top floor of a block on an East End estate where I had been staying with friends, so I just went over the roof, lifted out a skylight, and lowered myself in. I only had to change the locks and it was mine. But after just two or three days I came back to find a steel door fitted. You can't really squat alone; someone needs to be on the premises at all times or else the place can be reclaimed like this, without the need for a court order to get you out. I needed to get a team together.

The squatters' advice meeting was in a community hall in Kings Cross. I was the first enquiry of the session. Ivan was very much part of the Camden squatting scene, someone who squatted for political reasons rather than out of necessity. He was sat on a table swinging his legs as he waited for custom. He was dressed all in black; black boots, black jeans, a black leather cap and a motorcycle jacket with an anarchy symbol painted on the back. He said to wait and see if anyone else turned up, and soon we were joined by Erik, a tall Dutchman who told me he was working as a masseur. He said he had never squatted before and thought it would be exciting. I said I thought it would be exciting too, though probably not in a good way. Then Alan and Jerry showed up. They were living in a hostel for young homeless people and wanted out. Jerry was a skinny mixed-race teenager from Scotland, Alan was a short, stocky Glaswegian a few years older. They were both drunk. Alan told me he was a silver service waiter, and got out his waiter's knife to prove it. I felt faintly amused that he felt the need to do this; if I had got out a stethoscope, would that have made me a doctor? But there we were, a ragbag of people with no place to go, and no money.

Street life had changed beyond all recognition in

the few years I had been away. The old guard I had known, the street drinkers who had been on the streets for decades, had virtually all disappeared; a whole generation swept away. Typical homeless people now were in their twenties and hard at work on their own drug or alcohol problem, or were newly-arrived young immigrants, some legal, some not, trying to find ways to scrape a living in the anonymity of the city.

Ivan thought he could help. He was living in a street in Camden Town where half the street was squatted. There had been an eviction just days before, a few doors down from him. The place was pretty basic, he said, but it was there for the taking, and he had even lifted the fuses from the fuse box before the place had been boarded up. We went there later that evening, stopping off at a hardware shop on the way to pick up a spare Yale lock. Alan and Jerry went off to the local pub; this was not a job that needed all five of us and it felt like they would be more of a hindrance than a help. It was a breeze; the next-door neighbours were squatters so we just tapped on their door, walked through to their yard, hopped the wall and went in through the back.

When we had done the necessary, I stood in the doorway and looked out, and had a sudden shock of recognition. I knew this place. I had been here long before, on my very first week in London all those years before. This was the selfsame street where Sunset Strip had once been.

Once the place was secured Alan and Jerry returned from the pub, bringing three girls with them. It was impossible to avoid the observation that they appeared to be trying to collect a set. Karina was big, blonde and Swedish, Natalie was a medium-sized French redhead, and Elif was a tiny dark Turkish girl. They wanted to move in with us. It turned out they were all working together as waitresses for a chain that wasn't too picky about work permits, and paid accordingly, for only Natalie could work legally. They were all sharing a single small room on the premises, for which they were being charged most of their earnings. So then we were seven. I walked up to The Simon Community to blag a bin bag full of blankets. I didn't see anyone there I knew, and no one recognised me.

There were problems; it turned out that this squat was a non-starter. We had electricity but there was no water; the supply had been turned off in the street, not the house, and we had no idea how to get it back on. Any time we needed water we had to collect it by the bucketful from Ivan's. And then a few days later the builders turned up. Natalie had been on guard duty, and had done the right thing, not letting them in but talking to them from an upstairs window. But it turned out that the council had sold the place on for private development, and work was about to start.

We needed to find somewhere else quickly. I knew somewhere that might do; a big housing association place that had been empty for years, presumably waiting for funding that never seemed to come. But it would not be easy; it was on a busy street with a bank on one side and a long terraced row on the other, the ground floor windows were breeze-blocked, and the entrance secured with a hefty steel door.

We went at night, all four boys, and climbed the chain-link fence at the end of the terrace. We had about ten gardens and garden fences to get through without being seen. We decided to just rush through as quickly as we could, vaulting fences and clambering walls. If we had decided to check each garden first, making sure there were no possible observers looking out, it could have taken all night.

When we crossed the last wall into the yard we were aiming for, we were met by a huge muddy hole, like someone had been digging out a gas main. The earth had all been shovelled straight through the windows into the bathroom extension at the back of the house. The bath was full to the brim with mud, and the toilet bowl had been sledgehammered, its pieces scattered around the floor. This annoyed me; trashing a place to make it uninhabitable was not playing fair. We wandered through the house; it was otherwise good, there was even a bed left in every room. And then we went to have a look at the steelie from the inside. It was a monster of a door. Not good, I said, we'd have to hire a steel saw and bring it in through the back.

We decided to think more about it and go back the way we had come. I was first over the wall to the neighbouring yard, and froze. You've got to be kidding, I said. The house was all lit up, and through the uncurtained French windows I had a perfect view of a policeman still in uniform sitting and eating his dinner.

It could hardly have been less promising; the house had a policeman living on one side, and what appeared to be a half-finished attempt to tunnel into the bank on the other. Yet the next night, Erik turned up after work with a shrink-wrapped toilet bowl he had bought and carried back on the tube. I shook my head in exasperation. No, no, no, I said. You don't lay your eggs before you've built your nest.

I was round at Ivan's one evening drinking tea. Ivan was saying he felt terrible about having given us such bad advice. There were lots of other people around too, the house was always full of visitors, and an Australian girl overheard us and came over. She said she might know a place if we were desperate. Her and her friends had been evicted six weeks before from a big place up in Highgate. They had got two or three months out of it; it might tide us over for a few weeks if we were lucky, and give us a breathing space. The only thing she asked was if we decided to take it, her and her friends would like their fridge back; they had been caught by surprise by the bailiffs. As it turned out, we would not get a few weeks out of it; we would get a year.

I looked at Ivan and nodded. The others weren't around but I trusted myself more than I trusted them anyway. Ivan tossed me a spare helmet and handed me a holdall full of tools – jemmies, monkey wrenches, claw hammers, screwdrivers – everything you could possibly need for breaking and entry. Then we sped off up the Holloway Road. It was a cold night and I wasn't dressed for this, and the tool bag was so heavy it felt like it might rip my arm out of its socket.

We parked up around the corner and went the last hundred yards on foot. This was millionaires' row; huge detached houses in spacious grounds. The house was massive, towering high over the road from above a steeply sloping front garden. There was a long row of steps leading up to it, and there was no one about. There were a couple of lights on in upstairs rooms, but this didn't worry us; we guessed that the council had deliberately left them on to deter squatters. We were not deterred. We walked our way around the premises to look at our options. Every ground floor window was boarded up from the inside, and we didn't want to break glass unless we had a replacement pane to fit straight away. If we were spotted or heard, we needed to be on the premises, with our own locks fitted, and with no visible sign of entry, before the police got there. There were double doors front and back, but they were deadlocked and too exposed to view. But in the alley down one side of the house there was a side door that looked like it just had a Yale lock. We began to try to force it, charging at it like in a cop movie, but it had no give at all; it was like trying to open a wall, and all we were doing was bruising our shoulders.

Ivan thought we should give up and come back another time better prepared, but I wanted this house and I wanted it now. Beside the immobile door was a single tiny boarded-up window, much smaller than all the others. I could get through that, I said. I chipped away at the putty with a chisel, then pulled out the restraining pins with pliers. We carefully lifted out the undamaged pane and jemmied out the board inside. Ivan handed me a torch and gave me a leg up. See if you can get that door open for me, he said. I squeezed through the narrow gap. There was a crash as a plate hit the floor. I was standing on a fridge, which hummed into life the moment I stood on it. It was covered in dirty dishes. I hopped down and went over to the door, and the reason it had defeated us became clear; it had been nailed shut from the inside with rows of six-inch nails.

I looked around. I was in a large kitchen. There were more piles of washing up by the sink and a six-ring gas cooker. Off to one side was a huge walk-in pantry where I could see tubs of dried beans and lentils, sacks of potatoes and onions with foot-long sprouts, and other unidentifiable vegetables that had melted on the shelves. I told Ivan he would have to come in the same way; he passed me the tool bag then I helped drag him through the narrow gap. He got out a claw hammer and offered to start work on the door, while I took a torch and went to explore.

I opened the door to the next room, and froze in place. A huge dining table had been laid for about ten guests. A white tablecloth, candlesticks and vases of flowers, plates of food and glasses of wine at every seat. It was a ghost banquet. The air was stale and deathly, and with all the windows boarded there was no glimmer of light save for the thin beam of my torch which I flicked wildly around the room, trying to make sense of it all. I approached closer, reached out and touched the flowers in a vase. They crumbled at my touch, and a shower of dried rose petals fell to the table. I sniffed at a bottle of wine. The wine had turned to vinegar, and the food on the plates had turned to dust. The tablecloth was paper, and the table itself was just trestle tables pushed together. The Australian girl had said the bailiffs had come early; they must have come just as the residents were about to sit down to share their last supper. But for one brief moment I felt that I had entered another realm.

The house was vast; I had never been anywhere like it. Huge, high-ceilinged rooms with ornate cast-iron fire surrounds and marble mantelpieces. The house was carpeted wall to wall; I couldn't hear my own footsteps. Lobbies on every landing, with self-closing fire doors and meshed reinforced glass windows. There must have been close to fifteen bedrooms, and there was a bathroom on every floor, including one huge one that, bizarrely, contained two baths. Most of the rooms were furnished, with everything save for beds; there was not a single bed in the house, but there were sofas and armchairs, desks and chests of drawers and dressing tables. There was even a library, with bookshelves still lined with books.

Once we had freed the door and fitted it with our own lock, we put the little pane of glass back in place, held with pins for now. Ivan went back to tell the others; we had made enough noise for one night so the plan would be for the others to come tomorrow, and to bring some putty with them. So for this one night I had the place to myself. I wouldn't turn on any lights for now; I would wait until we were all moved in. It was a cold night so I lit the gas oven and threw open the doors, then got a chair from the dining room and parked myself in front of it. I could sleep on the sofa later, or if it was too cold just stay in my chair by the oven. I was hungry so I checked the pantry for anything salvageable, and ended up frying myself some potatoes and garlic, and putting on a pan of water for tea.

It was impossible to resist exploring the house further; I could scarcely believe the place. In one little room I found a filing cabinet full of files stamped Confidential. The place had been used as a children's home, but had been closed in the cuts. They must have left at short notice if they hadn't even taken all the paperwork with them. The library was all children's books. I pulled out one and opened it: a Ladybird Book about homes. On a double spread were two pictures of the same room. In the first, it was completely empty; bare boards, a window without curtains. In the other there was a Janet and John style family sitting on a sofa smiling happily, a dog curled up asleep on a rug in front of a blazing fire. An empty house is not a home, it said. People make a house into a home.

Over the course of the next day the others drifted up from Camden and I proudly showed them around, and the house stumbled into life. The police turned up on day two and demanded to be let in when we wouldn't open the door for them. We repelled them with a Section 6 notice pushed through the letter box. Legal Warning: this is our home now and we intend to stay here. There is always at least one person on the premises. Any attempt to enter by violence or by threatening violence is a criminal offence. And so on. One young constable said he was going to break the door down anyway, but an older, more experienced officer told him it wasn't worth it. They left, grumbling, and said they would make sure the council got a court order as soon as possible.

I felt we had a duty to fill all the rooms, there were so many still empty. Others were more reluctant, thinking we should keep it to ourselves, and I was outvoted. But exceptions were made almost straight away, and the house began to fill. Amy and Neville were a young couple who were expecting a baby – they met in a hostel for the homeless, but when they got together had been told that the hostel didn't accept couples, and the local housing office had told them to come back when they had either a baby or an eviction notice to show for themselves. They were in an anomalous position: while the rest of us dreaded eviction, they were hoping to be evicted as soon as possible. A couple of the other girls got themselves boyfriends; the kind of boyfriends who didn't have anywhere else to live. And then, once the precedent had been set, I moved in some friends of mine, visa-less, who had been struggling to make enough in the shadowland of the black economy to make ends meet.

People found what work they could. Alan would get jobs not as a silver service waiter but as a barman. I don't know if he dipped his fingers in the till, if he drank away the profits, or if he simply couldn't count, because he would never explain why he was fired from every single job after no more than two days. Mohammed was the most ambitious; he would try his luck at building sites posing as Pierre, a Frenchman, and would usually get a week or two before his national insurance number was rejected as bogus. On one occasion he managed to pull off a job as head chef at a French restaurant. He lasted nearly two weeks by just telling everyone else what to do, until one day, in a moment of boredom, he was caught chopping an onion and it became immediately apparent that he had never worked in a restaurant in his entire life. His inventiveness was admirable, though of course you wouldn't ever want to trust someone who was quite so good at lying.

It was easier for me, being legal. I signed up with an agency and would phone them up each day from the local phone box to see if they had anything for me. I would take anything; start being picky with an agency and the offers soon dry up. It would always be the shifts that no one else wanted. At a moment's notice I would have to drop everything and travel out to the far reaches of London. Weekend shifts, night shifts, bank holidays; on one occasion forty-eight consecutive hours. I gave the agency just one condition; no strike-breaking.

Throw a disparate group of people into close proximity, and of course there will be tensions. The main source of irritation was Alan. He would arrive home drunk in the middle of the night and stagger around the house, walking in to people's rooms and waking them up, for company I think. Three in the morning and he would walk into my room, shake me awake and ask for a cigarette.

Alan, it's the middle of the night, I'm sleeping, will you get the fuck out of my room?

I just need a cigarette.

If I give you a cigarette will you get the hell out?

I give him a cigarette paper and a pinch of tobacco. He starts to make it, incredibly slowly, until I grab it back off him and finish the job, then he sits at the end of my bed and starts to talk, and talk.

I interrupt him. Alan, if you don't get out right now I will have no choice but to punch you in the face. And then I get up and manhandle him to the door. He may well be back later for a repeat performance. It is annoying enough for me; worse for the girls.

I loved my room. Rooms before had always been neither here nor there to me; there had been so many of them and they were just somewhere to park myself when I needed to sleep. It was an attic room with no corners, just sweeping white curves. It was the best room in the house, but I was first in so I got first pick. There was a small abandoned dressing table, and a little washbasin and mirror. There was a spider plant in a pot, the only plant hardy enough to be rescued after six weeks without water or light. Otherwise there was no furniture; just my bedroll spread out by the fireplace.

From the windows of the third floor there was a fine view up the hill to the Alexandra Palace transmitter, and just outside was a huge ornamental pine, taller than the house. Sometimes at night the lights from a car turning on the hill outside would pierce the windows and send shadow branches racing across the ceiling and around the walls. On one of my first nights there, as I lay in my sleeping bag with my head by the fireplace, I was woken by a spectral wailing that echoed down the chimney as if amplified, loud enough to make me sit bolt upright. There was a second tawny owl on my windowsill, seemingly peering in, and I watched as it flew silently up into the pine, where it was joined by its mate from the chimney pot.

I would sit on the dressing table, which was the closest thing I had to a chair, and look out. Fox trails wound through the overgrown grass beneath. There were goldcrests in the pine, tiny, yellow-capped and restless, and sometimes there would be the blue flashes of a family of jays. I got myself a nut-feeder and attached it to a length of string, then tossed it over a nearby branch and tied the end to the window latch. It looked like I was fishing for birds.

One Last Thing
1989

THEY CAME in the night, mob-handed. They told us they were moving in whether we liked it or not, and that if we tried to stop them they would come back with their twenty-seven mates and break every window in the place. Why twenty-seven, I don't know, but it was actually about right; over the course of the next few months there probably were about twenty-seven strangers in the house at one point or another. They were right about the windows too; by the time the squat finally died there was barely a pane intact.

I was out working the night they arrived, but a friend from out of town was sleeping in my bed, and she later told me they had burst into the room at dead of night, shadow-boxing and making shapes like a bunch of drunken ninjas. I had a panicky call at work from Erik, telling me there was big trouble and I needed to get back right away, but I was miles away and couldn't walk out on a job. By the time I did get back it was all settled. Resistance was futile.

Many of the group came and went as they fell in and out of favour, but the core of three became a permanent fixture in the old library on the ground floor, and came in and out through the windows so no one would know if they were home. Two of them were brothers. Joe, the older brother, was a hulking, heavily-muscled young man with a crew cut. He looked like a squaddie, but of course this was a prison haircut, and jailhouse gym muscles. Joe barely spoke; he never said anything to me apart from, All right Neil? every time we passed one another in the corridor. Dave was just as big but more presentable and communicative; he did the talking for both of them. The third member of the crew was Anna, Joe's girlfriend. She was about ten years older than him, and seemed to have a bottle of vodka permanently fixed to her hand.

So, they moved in to the library and set up in business dealing dope. Pills too, morphine sulphate and Valium, though at first Dave didn't even know what he had on his hands. He had to ask around to find out what they were, and what they were worth.

He started trying to tell me the story of how they had been snatched from a local hospital, but I cut him short: Whoa there, I said, I really don't want to know. They had other sidelines too; once as I walked past their open door I got a glimpse of a whole stack of stereos, probably about ten of them.

It was all Alan's fault. I know this because for several days Alan wandered the house hanging his head and saying, It's all my fault. A lot of the time Elif would be close behind him, pointing her finger and saying, You're so stupid, Alan. Sooo bloody stupid. She was incensed. It turned out that Alan had shot his mouth off after a long session in the local pub. That was all it took.

The asset-stripping started soon after. Some of the ground-floor fireplaces and fire-surrounds were ripped out, dragged through the house in a trail of brick dust and plaster, and sold on to a shop. A few days later I returned to find one of Joe and Dave's mates sat at the top of the garden steps with the biggest prize of all, the huge marble-topped fire-surround from the living room. I went in and mentioned it to Alan and Jerry in the kitchen. Alan turned pale and said, They can't do that. That's police evidence. And then he rushed out.

When he got back I demanded an explanation. It turned out that Alan and Neville had decided to get a piece of the action before it was too late. They had gone round the house and ripped out every remaining fireplace. Karina was away, and they had even smashed open the padlock to her door and made a mess of her room in their rush to get the job done while everyone was out. They had been halfway down the stairs with the last one, Alan and Neville at one end, the sheepskin-clad man from the shop at the other, when the police walked in. The shop guy dropped his end, gave a hurt look, and said, What, lads, you mean this isn't kosher?

The police took all the fireplaces off in their van, to be used in evidence; all save the one from the living room, which was just too big for the van, and was left stranded in the middle of the room with an evidence tag attached. Neville was pretty bullish about the whole thing; he figured that with a pregnant girlfriend he was relatively safe. But Alan was convinced he was going down, so much so that he went off and got himself a live-in job in a pub.

I ran into Alan one more time, months later. I was

in a pub in Brixton when he came in looking for work. He looked pleased to see me and came over to blag a roll-up and half a pint. He told me it was getting harder and harder for him to find work; just about every chain in London had banned him now. I didn't ask why. He had a new place, he said, I should call round some time and we could catch up properly. He went and got paper and pen from behind the bar and wrote down his address for me. Then he went quiet for a while, looked down at the table, and mumbled, It was all my fault. Like a mantra. When he was gone I screwed up the piece of paper and threw it in the ashtray. I never saw him again.

Amy was heavily pregnant now and seldom went out. She would spend her mornings sitting on the bottom step of the stairs, waiting for the postman to arrive, and as I mostly worked lates I would sometimes join her. The library was right by the front door, and if there was no one on watch the post would disappear into a room and never be seen again. Obviously Amy didn't want to lose a giro, but most of all she didn't want to miss an eviction order. Her big fear was of having her baby taken off her at birth, and I tried to reassure her that this would never happen. The letterbox flapped open and she went over, picked up a card, laughed, and brought it over to show me. It was for Alan, from the local library. His copy of *How to Win Friends and Influence People* was now three months overdue.

The next to get himself in a whole heap of trouble was Jerry. It was bound to happen; Jerry was one of these people who never have any money at all, and spend their life hovering as close as possible to those who do. Whenever anyone in the squat lit up a joint, within seconds Jerry would silently appear at their shoulder, like a smiling shadow. It was uncanny. Our new arrivals had dope and beer and money, and from the moment of their arrival he tried to insinuate himself into their favour. It was never going to end well, and when Anna claimed that Jerry had made a drunken pass at her after sharing her vodka when the boys were out, he had to do a runner. Joe and Dave cleaned out his room, confiscated everything, so that if he tried to come back for his stuff he would have to get past them first.

Most people in the squat were incredulous at the

allegation; Anna was almost twice his age, and twice his size. But I wasn't so sure; Jerry was second only to Alan in his ability to do really, really stupid things while drunk. I was sure we would not be seeing Jerry again, but I was wrong.

He turned up a few days later, looking exhausted and dishevelled; he had been unable to find anywhere to stay and had been sleeping rough. We were all getting ready to go out, for just about the only collective activity we ever engaged in. Erik was leaving, not just leaving the squat but leaving the country, and we were giving him a send-off. Good for him; he didn't really belong in this world anyway. When we got to the local pub, Joe and Dave were already in there, acting like they didn't know us; it was starting to look like it would be an interesting night.

Jerry got up and went to the pub toilets. A few moments later, Joe got up from his table and followed him in. We all stopped talking and looked at each other. I'll go, I said eventually. I walked over and opened the door to see Joe had Jerry pinned against the wall, one massive hand around his neck, Jerry's feet dangling off the floor. It was kind of impressive. It had an almost filmic quality. Jerry didn't look scared, he looked resigned, and that was impressive too, in its own way. Joe turned to me as I opened the door and said, All right, Neil? And then he looked suddenly deflated, or tired of it all, as if his rage was spent, and he lowered Jerry gently to the ground.

It is an annoyance when you return from a long shift at work to find a police cordon in your street, the squeal and throb of acid house beats in the air, and a bouncer at your door trying to charge you a fiver to get into your own home. Of course, I am playing a little fast and loose here with the words 'own' and 'home'. This was a time when any available space could be turned at a moment's notice into a party venue. And there they were, those who had managed to get past the police line, some of them even shinning up drainpipes and hammering on upstairs windows to try to escape the door charge.

It turned out that Dave had sold the place for fifty quid to a party promoter he had met in the pub, and then made sure he was out for the night to escape the flak, not telling anyone at all, not even his own brother. It was so brazen it was almost comical. The acts of violence were not so funny. This is an essential fact of street life that is not always visible to those on the outside, and rarely spills over to the world at large. It is brutal, run by straw bosses who are powerless in society's terms but who rule the streets by intimidation and the constant threat of violence. I have known people be killed over a five pound drug debt. But that was later, in another place, when crack came to town. Everything had stepped up a gear, and nothing would ever be quite the same again.

The fighting would usually start around midnight, after everyone had got back from a night's drinking. This was the norm, not the exception. This may seem like an exaggeration, but it really was several nights a week. More and more people would get sucked into these battles as the night wore on. I kept my head down and kept out of it, but it was relatively easy for me. I had a life outside the squat, work and old friends, and the only people in the squat I spent much time with socially were the couple I had known before. But there were many others in the house, newly-arrived in town, or in the country, who didn't have much of a life outside of it; this was their world. The shouting went on, allegations and counter-allegations; who owed money to whom, who had robbed from whom, who had slept with whom, until at some point at two or three in the morning a crescendo would be reached, and Joe or Dave would put a fist, or perhaps someone's head, through a window. Often, when morning came, one of their 'friends' would no longer be living in the house. It was impossible to keep up with it.

One particular night, one of their friends must have caused particular offence, for Joe and Dave set about trashing his room. They would demolish it so thoroughly that no one ever used it again. Not long after the noise finally died down, my door was flung open and a torchlight shone in my eyes. There were two police officers standing behind the beam; the police could wander in at will now, for the double doors that led from the living room to the back garden had long since been ripped off their hinges. They said that the neighbours had reported loud crashes coming from the premises.

I just got in, I said.

I was asleep, said the woman in bed beside me.

Let's get out of here, said one officer to the other,

Everyone in this place is deaf.

I got up to take a look at the damage. It was spectacular. I ran into Dave, he couldn't stop laughing. He said that he had only just been able to sweep all his pills under his mattress in time. There was a strange glint in his eyes; he was not high on his own supply for he never touched the stuff, he was high on violence.

The squat was in its dying days now. The kitchen was flooded and no one ever bothered to put out the rubbish any more; piles of maggoty waste overflowed from the kitchen bin. And still the eviction notice didn't come. The house was full of strangers that came and went seemingly at random; there was no point in even trying to put names to faces. On more than one occasion I came in to find a prostitute servicing a client in my room. Theft was rife; anything you wanted to see again you had to carry with you. When I went to work I would pack a carrier bag with towel, soap, toothbrush and spare clothes. None of these things were safe to leave. People claimed that even their dirty laundry had gone missing. On one occasion every clock in the house vanished. Jerry finally found three alarm clocks tossed in the long grass in the back garden. All of them had been overwound until their springs had broken.

When the house had first been invaded, padlocks had begun to proliferate on doors, until finally there was a lock on every room save mine. I thought this was a mistake. A padlock was an advertisement, both that you were out and that you had something worth taking. They were like a challenge; they almost demanded to be broken open, and were, with unremitting regularity. I didn't bother to lock my door, so that people could see for themselves that I had nothing worth taking. Better to have nothing, for then you have nothing to lose. But I was wrong. I did have something; I had one last thing.

Almost a decade before, back at the Simon Community, I had come in to the house one day to find Gypsy Davy sat on the sofa, wrapped in a blanket and with his battered trilby tipped back on his head. He waved at me to come over. He had been sitting right at the end of the sofa where he had a view of the door; I had the distinct impression that he had been waiting for me.

What's the matter, Davy, are you ill? I said.

In reply he got out a blood-spotted handkerchief, and coughed more blood into it. When he had finally stopped coughing, he said, You knew Casey, didn't you?

I did, I replied. He was a good man.

He was. Look at this.

He reached into his pocket, got out an old cross and chain, and handed it to me. I turned it in my hands. It was an ugly thing, stainless steel with an X scored across the centre to mark it as a Catholic crucifix.

I remember this, I said. Casey was wearing it the first time we met.

He gave it to me just before he died, Davy said. I want you to have it.

I shook my head and held it out to him. I can't take this. I barely knew the man.

Gypsy Davy reached out and curled my fingers over the cross. You know me, he said, I'll just get drunk and lose it. He gave it to me, and now I'm giving it to you. That's the way it is.

Soon after that day Gypsy Davy was taken to hospital. He never came out again. I had carried the cross everywhere with me for ten years. It had climbed mountains with me, crossed deserts and oceans. That cross was the best part of me, my last reminder of a time when I still liked myself. And now it was gone. I had left it hanging from a nail on the wall of my room.

I went round the house asking everybody I could find, but I knew it was pointless. I knew just where I had to go. Finally I knocked on the door of the library; Anna answered and invited me in. She was alone with her bottle. It was the first time I had been in the library since the day they had moved in. I told her I had lost something, told her it had been given to me by a friend just before he had died, and made a deliberate point of mentioning that it was stainless steel and totally valueless to anyone else.

Joe and Dave came in through the window.

All right, Neil? Joe asked.

Dave looked at me suspiciously. What's he doing here?

Anna explained that I was looking for something I had lost. Dave still didn't look happy. Well, why's he asking us then? It's nothing to do with us.

I'm asking everybody in the house if they've seen it, I said, and then I began to tell them the story, and they sat and listened.

After I had finished, there was a long pause. Finally, Anna spoke. We haven't got it, but I've got an idea who might. I'll see what I can do.

The following morning the cross was hanging by its chain from the handle of my door. I had appealed to their better nature, and found that they actually had one.

The Keeper of Memory
1989

THE FOLLOWING MORNING I rose early, my bag already packed, and took the tube to Brent Cross. Then I walked along the North Circular to the start of the M1. I had come this way many times before over the years, through a bleak landscape of flyovers and roundabouts, of concrete buttresses and lost hubcaps, of dead space and scrapyards and blackening gravel. As I walked beneath a slip road I looked out for the old man. He had always been there, every time I had come this way, year after year, with his long beard and his overcoat tied on with string, and I would always greet him, though he would never reply. He had built a lean-to out of wooden pallets and plastic sheeting, behind a torn chain-link fence and propped against the concrete pillar that supported the slip road above. It always struck me as a strange choice of a place to make your home, with the deafening roar of traffic

from every direction and the air thick with exhaust
fumes. But now it looked like he had gone; his shelter
had collapsed and there was no sign of a recent fire.
Not much to leave behind.

There were already nine or ten people waiting at
the foot of the motorway; it was always busy here. I
walked the line and placed myself the required twenty
yards beyond the last person in the queue. As I passed
the other hitchhikers I nodded in greeting to each of
them. Few of them responded, not welcoming the
additional competition. This first wait would often be
the longest of the day. Drivers would not pick people
up in order of arrival, but would stop for whoever
they chose, so you could be stranded here for hours.
With so many of us, we were sprawled well up the
hard shoulder, so the police could arrive at any time
and clear us off. It is frustrating to have a very long
wait before you have even started, especially if you
see someone arrive hours after you and get picked up
almost immediately. But on this occasion I didn't do
too badly; it was less than two hours before a truck
pulled over and I was able to set off.

My hope had been that on that first day I would

make it out of England and through to the Scottish Borders. In the event I did better than I had hoped; I made it clear through Glasgow before nightfall, and on a little further, to Dumbarton. I stopped off for a bag of chips, and then walked to the edge of town to look for a suitable spot to wait. But there was nothing doing; there was very little traffic and people are reluctant to pick you up late in the day. Eventually, to stave off boredom, I decided to start walking. Fewer and fewer cars were passing now, and hitching while walking doesn't usually work; much of the time you are not in a place where drivers can get a good enough look at you to make up their minds before it's too late to stop. I walked for two or three hours, until I was far out in the countryside, nothing but fields and trees all around. It was dark and there was no traffic; it was time to start looking for a place to sleep.

Then I saw the mattress at the side of the road. It seemed almost new, as if it had fallen off the back of a lorry rather than having been fly-tipped. A mattress in the middle of nowhere, just as I was thinking about settling down somewhere for the night; it seemed too good to be true. Over the roadside ditch and the barbed wire fence was a little copse of oak trees at the edge of a field, so I tossed the mattress across the fence and clambered over after it. I could just make out a cow far away across the field so I checked the ground for cowpats. It seemed to be clear, so I positioned the mattress close to the trunk of a big old oak, where I would get as much shelter as possible if it started to rain. Then I unrolled my sleeping bag and went to sleep, thinking myself lucky.

At some point in the night I woke to a noise; a kind of snorting. I sat up in my sleeping bag. It looked as though a cow had wandered over to inspect me. Shoo, I said. It looked massive silhouetted against the starry sky. I looked more carefully; it had massive horns, a thick ring through its nose, and it was pawing at the ground with one of its forelegs. I have never moved so fast in my life; I would not have imagined it possible to exit a zipped up sleeping bag in such a brief instant. I made it behind the trunk of the oak tree just as the bull charged. It lunged at me from one side of the tree, and then the other, but thankfully I had camped beneath the tree with broadest trunk. It tried to chase me around the tree, but by shimmying around the oak pressed close to the wood, I was able to circuit the tree quicker than the beast.

The bull was getting frustrated. It stood facing me, huge and black, its forelegs splayed a little, snorting great clouds of steam from its nostrils. With a flick of its head, it tossed my sleeping bag into the air and left it hanging suspended from an overhead branch. It managed to get one of the arm straps of my pack looped around a horn, and this drove it into a frenzy; it ran around in circles, shaking its head and sending the contents of the bag scattering in all directions. Seeing my chance while it was distracted, I made a run for it and vaulted over the fence.

Though I was relieved to be out on the road with a barbed wire fence between me and the bull, my problems were not over yet; I still had to recover all my belongings, including my clothes. It had been a mild night and I had stripped down to just my boxer shorts. I was alive to the ridiculousness of my situation. Less than a year before, I had been travelling alone in Africa, camping wild and tentless. I had learned to keep a little campfire burning through the night, to deter the leopards and hyenas. I had learned to wrap any food I was carrying in layer upon layer of plastic and suspend it with string from the branch of a nearby tree. And I had learned never, ever, to take oranges anywhere that there might be an elephant. Yet as it turned out, my closest ever encounter with a dangerous animal would be here in a farmer's field in Dunbartonshire.

So I stood and watched and waited as the furious bull gored the stuffing out of the mattress. It began to rain, a persistent drizzle rather than a heavy shower; I would have been all right under my tree. I saw a car approaching, the beam of its headlights piercing through the raindrops. The driver didn't stop; under the circumstances I don't suppose I would have stopped either. The middle of the night, the middle of the countryside, a man standing in the rain naked save for his underpants.

Eventually the bull's anger was spent, and he stomped off across the field. I crept over the fence and gathered up what belongings I could find in the dark. I had lost any inclination to sleep so I set off walking through the night. There was no traffic at all. At first light I found myself alongside a loch, and the midges began to get unbearable. I came to a phone box and took shelter in it for a while; I even managed to doze off for a few minutes, propped up in a standing position. Once the sun had risen over the loch, the midges began to settle, and I set off walking again. I was offered a lift by the first vehicle to come by. It was a post van. We made ridiculously slow progress as the postman had to stop off at every house we passed, but I wasn't complaining.

I made it to the ferry terminal at Kennacraig by mid-afternoon, in time for the daily ferry to Port Askaig on the northern tip of Islay. After the two-hour crossing it would be just a five minute hop across the Sound. While I waited for the little car ferry to take me on that last leg I sat on the harbour wall beside the jetty and watched the black guillemots that were nesting in niches in the sea wall beneath me. And I looked over the Sound to the Isle of Jura. The Paps of Jura, domes of bare granite, shone in the afternoon sun and really did look breast-like, as if the island was a sleeping giantess.

Hitching on Jura is not like hitching anywhere else I have ever been. The island may have only a handful of inhabitants, and traffic may be sparse, to say the least. But on Jura, no driver has ever passed me by. They may only be going two hundred yards up the road, but without fail they have stopped and offered me a ride anyway.

I called in at the shop in Craighouse, to stock up with a few bare essentials. Coffee and sugar, the makings of a few sandwiches, some instant noodles. I then continued, hop by short hop, up the island's relatively sheltered east coast. On my way, I looked out for the little cluster of birches where I had camped five years before, and the house where I had been made welcome.

I made the roadhead beyond Ardlussa just before nightfall. It was raining now, a hard soaking rain, not the drizzle of the night before. I would need shelter. Set back from the road, in a bracken-filled field, was a shed. It looked just like a garden shed that had somehow got lost; I could see no reason why it should be there. But it was unlocked, it was empty, and it was rainproof. It was just large enough to lay out my sleeping bag for the night. And that night, no animals came to disturb my sleep.

Though the road ended here, it was still another ten miles to the northern tip of the island. To start with, there was a rutted dirt track that was easy to follow. It led, after five miles or so, to Barnhill, a whitewashed stone house with a black roof on the hillside overlooking the sea, that was once home to Jura's most famous resident. In 1946, George Orwell came to live here with his adopted son, in spite of his failing health, in spite, or perhaps because, of its impeccable remoteness. Here, at an upstairs window looking out at a fine view over the sea to the mainland, he wrote what would be his last book, *Nineteen Eighty-Four*. As soon as the book was completed, his health deteriorated still further, and he was forced to return to London where he died soon after of TB.

There was just one more house beyond Barnhill; after that, there would be no more occupied dwellings for thirty or forty miles of coastline. I followed the rocky shoreline now, skipping from boulder to boulder. Everywhere there were crab shells, left tidily on the highest rocks, neatly eviscerated by otters.

At the northernmost point of my journey, I stopped and looked out over the Gulf of Corryvreckan to the

uninhabited Isle of Scarba. It was relatively calm
now, but in the tidal race the waters surge around
an underwater pinnacle to form one of the largest
whirlpools in the world. Notoriously, Orwell almost
lost his life here. With his foster son and guests, he
had been on a trip to the western shores of the island.
On their return, they misjudged the tides and their
outboard motor was wrenched away by the force of
the waves. They managed to scramble onto a rocky
islet in the gulf just as their boat capsized, and they
were later rescued by a lobster fisherman.

I left the northern shore of the island and made my
way to the wild west coast. These were trackless wastes
now; there was no path to follow, just occasionally
a deer trail through the bracken. This was a broken
landscape of arches and stacks, of cliffs and caves and
amphitheatres. For much of the way there was a raised
beach high above the waterline. In the last Ice Age,
everything here had been subsumed by an ice sheet
three miles deep. When the ice finally melted away,
the land, freed from this enormous burden, had risen,
and the south coast of England had correspondingly
sunk into the sea. A weight of water sufficient to tilt

and pivot an entire landmass.

So these caves a hundred feet above the shore had all once been sea caves. Each time I came to another, I would take a look inside; I thought I might find one suitable for sleeping in. But inside they were mounded high with piles of earth and scattered with deer droppings. In one cave I surprised a red deer stag; it raced in circles around the walls, a fire of panic in its eyes, until I backed away from the entrance so it could make its escape. I realised that these mounds of earth, some ten or more feet high, were made entirely from the dung of generation after generation of deer. The red deer had probably been using these caves for shelter from winter storms since long before the very first Picts had made it across the water and settled the island.

The skeletons were in another, smaller, cave. A pair of otters; I guessed from their size that they had been almost fully grown cubs. Perhaps their mother had died, or had abandoned them, and they had waited and waited, calling out for salvation that never came. No predator had ever come and scattered these bones. Their flesh and fur must have just slowly sifted down into the dirt. I imagined that this must have been the exact spot where they had lived and died. They had never been disturbed by man nor beast, and I could still see the frozen moment of their death. They were curled up together, side by side, as if in a last embrace. I left them where they lay.

Soon after, I saw my first live otter of this trip, even though it was still only mid-afternoon. From this point on I would see several each day. It was in a little cove, a crescent of white sand, and it was padding along the waterline leaving a neat trail of footprints as it went. It must have heard me, or scented me, for it paused and looked me over, then carried on its way without quickening its pace. I followed its footprints along the sand. It was a delightful little bay; a rocky promontory twisted round to the north and almost enclosed it. The water in the pool it formed was shallow and calm, almost waveless, creating a little sheltered harbour not much larger than the size of a swimming pool. I decided that it was the perfect spot for a swim, so I stripped off and waded in. I had swum about halfway across when a head rose out the water right in front of me, just a few feet away. It was a grey seal, about the same size as me, and it watched me patiently with moist, unblinking eyes.

I could have walked on for the remaining hours of daylight, but I decided this was a perfect place to stop for the night, and I had no schedule to keep, no deadlines to meet. The cove was well sheltered, surrounded by cliffs on three sides, and the sky was clear. I knew this could quickly change, but there were caves that I could resort to sheltering in if I had no choice. There was a little stream that tumbled over the cliffs in a waterfall, and wound through the sands to the sea, so I would have fresh water. I found a level grassy spot beside the stream and lay out my groundsheet and sleeping bag. Then I built a little circle of stones from the raised beach above, and gathered up some driftwood. I got my fire lit for the night and set some water to boil in an empty tin can.

That night as I lay in my sleeping bag and looked up at the stars I realised that it was over twenty-four hours since I had last seen another person. This was one of the first times in my life that I could honestly say this, and it felt good.

For two more days I continued my way down the

coast. I came to long deserted bays of windswept sand, and rocky shores where I had to clamber from one boulder to the next. Where the land rose more gently from the sea, there would be raised shingle beaches far up on the moor. I found myself walking through a vast colony of nesting common gulls. Whoever named the gulls must have been here in Scotland, for these are actually one of the least numerous of our gulls. Their nests were clustered close together, just out of each other's pecking range. As I picked my way between them the nearby birds started to clamour, and their calls spread like a wave through the colony, until the whole hillside was a cacophony of alarm. But the birds stuck to their nests; as with island life the world over, the wildlife here seemed preternaturally tame. The only obvious exception was the red deer; used to being hunted, they were constantly wary and alert. In places the cliffs made the shoreline impassable and I was forced up onto the hills. I found a bare landscape of rock and heather, studded with tiny lochans. Herds of red deer would be retreating over the ridges as I walked. Stumbling onto a tiny hidden tarn, I found a nesting pair of red-throated divers, primitive looking birds that swam low in the water and seemed not to mind my sitting close by to watch them. They looked beautiful in their summer dress; I had only seen them before in their drab winter costume.

Following a deer trail that led over a ridge through deep bracken, I came upon a cast-off antler and picked it up for a closer look. It was a four-pointer. If I remembered correctly the stags grew an extra tine on their antlers for each year of their lives. It was in perfect condition save for a chip missing from the tip of one point. I imagined this as a battle scar; I pictured it having been inflicted when it had locked horns with another stag during the rut of the previous autumn. It was a beautiful object and I decided to hold on to it as a keepsake, so I thrust it through the straps of my pack before I continued on my way.

Finally I came to a little bothy close to the shore, and decided I would take advantage of its shelter and stay here for a couple of nights. If there had been anyone else staying I would probably have carried on my way, but it was clearly unoccupied. It was beautifully situated where the west coast met a big sea loch that almost bisected the island. There were views across the loch to the Paps on the southern end of the island. There was a little bay that seemed to have the perfect aspect to capture vast quantities of driftwood, a whole forest of it, far more than you could ever need. I speculated on where all this wood had come from, if some of it had come from across the sea in Ireland, or even if any of it might have followed the Gulf Stream all the way from the Americas. Right in front of it was a little pool of fresh water, and that evening I sat in the doorway and watched in the gloaming, the long drawn-out half-light of the northern nights, as the otters came out to play. These coastal otters may feed entirely in the sea, but they still rely on the presence of fresh water where they can wash the salt from their fur. I watched them until it was too dark to see, then went in for the night, and sat on the camp bed by my driftwood fire.

In the morning I went for a gentle stroll along the beach; it was a pleasure to walk unencumbered by a backpack. While I was out I heard a gunshot from somewhere in the hills. As I walked back I saw a little boat tied up in the bay, and the silhouettes of three men on the ridgeline above, the first people I had seen in three days. I arrived back at the bothy at the same time as one of these men; an elderly Scotsman with a deerstalker hat and a rifle slung over his shoulder. He looked surprised to see me, cross even, and demanded to know what I was doing there. I told him I was walking the coast and had stopped overnight in the bothy. He grunted and walked away.

I went in and relit my fire, and soon had another visitor. This was a much younger man, very well-spoken and with an expensive looking camera slung around his neck. He asked if he could come in and join me, and I said of course, and added that there was plenty of room if they all wanted to stay. He said no, they were going to head further along the coast shortly. He talked and talked; after the days of silence it came almost as a shock. He was here with his father and a guide, he told me, and then he started a discussion about how wonderful the wildlife was on the island. He didn't really agree with hunting, he said, his passion was photography.

I wondered why he was telling me all this, and then suddenly I got it. They were stalking out of season; the open season for red deer didn't start for another month. I imagined that this young man had been sent to keep me occupied while the other two loaded their trophy into the boat. Eventually my visitor bid me farewell and shook my hand. I watched as their boat puttered away to the south until it was lost to view.

The following morning I set off walking again; I wanted to be away from the chance of meeting people again. Eventually I found the place. It was a beautiful spot on a rocky promontory facing out to sea; a place that I would always imagine I would want to come back to. I sat in the shelter of the little cairn; the wind was picking up and it was starting to spot with rain. I decided this was as good a place as any and started to dismantle one side of the cairn; the side that faced out west to the sea.

I got out the old cross from my pocket. After burying it in the heart of the cairn I carefully replaced all the rocks I had removed. There was no real sense to what I was doing; I knew that the dead have no expectations of us. The cross had no meaning for me as a religious symbol. No one gained from what I was doing. But I had made a promise that I would keep the cross safe, and the way my life was going it felt as though the only safe place was a place with no people. I assumed that one day I would come back for it, when my life was more secure. But if there is one thing life has taught me, it is that there is no such thing as security. Security is an illusion. Everything you have can be snatched away in an instant. And I have come to realise that what I was really being asked to keep safe was a memory, not a physical object. Memories are the only things we can truly own, and even they slip from our grasp if we don't handle them with care.

It took me three days to get back to London; a day of walking and two days of hitching. I walked along the shore of a sea loch back to the road on the east coast of the island. I camped out in the shelter of a little stand of conifers by the sea, and watched the otters at nightfall one last time. On my journey back, one of my drivers even put me up for the night on a sofa in Glasgow. I was used to this happening when hitching in a big country like America, but this was the first time I had ever been accommodated while hitching in Britain.

Packed away in my bag was a memento; the cast

off red deer antler I had stumbled over in the bracken. I don't know what became of it, I must have left it somewhere along the way. The course of my life has not been very conducive to keeping hold of things.

First published in 2013 by Little Toller Books
Lower Dairy, Toller Fratrum, Dorset

Text © Neil Ansell 2013
Illustrations © Jonny Hannah 2013

Set in Plantin Light by Little Toller Books
Printed on Munken papers

All papers used by Little Toller Books are natural,
recyclable products made from wood grown
in sustainable, well-managed forests

A CIP catalogue record for this book is
available from the British Library

ISBN 978-1-908213-13-6

1 3 5 7 9 8 6 4 2